What Do You Need?

Seed
Learning

What do you need?

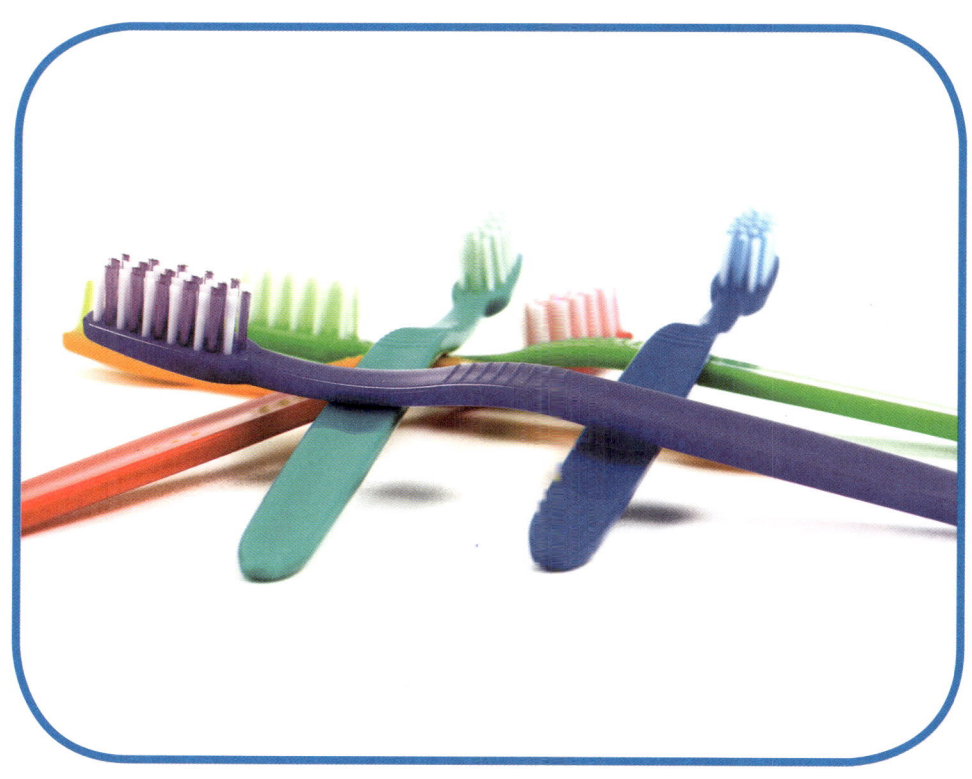

I need
toothbrushes.

I need four
toothbrushes.

What do you need?

I need bandages.

I need five
bandages.

What do you need?

I need straws.

I need six straws.

What do you need?

I need stickers.

I need seven stickers.

What do you need?

I need buttons.

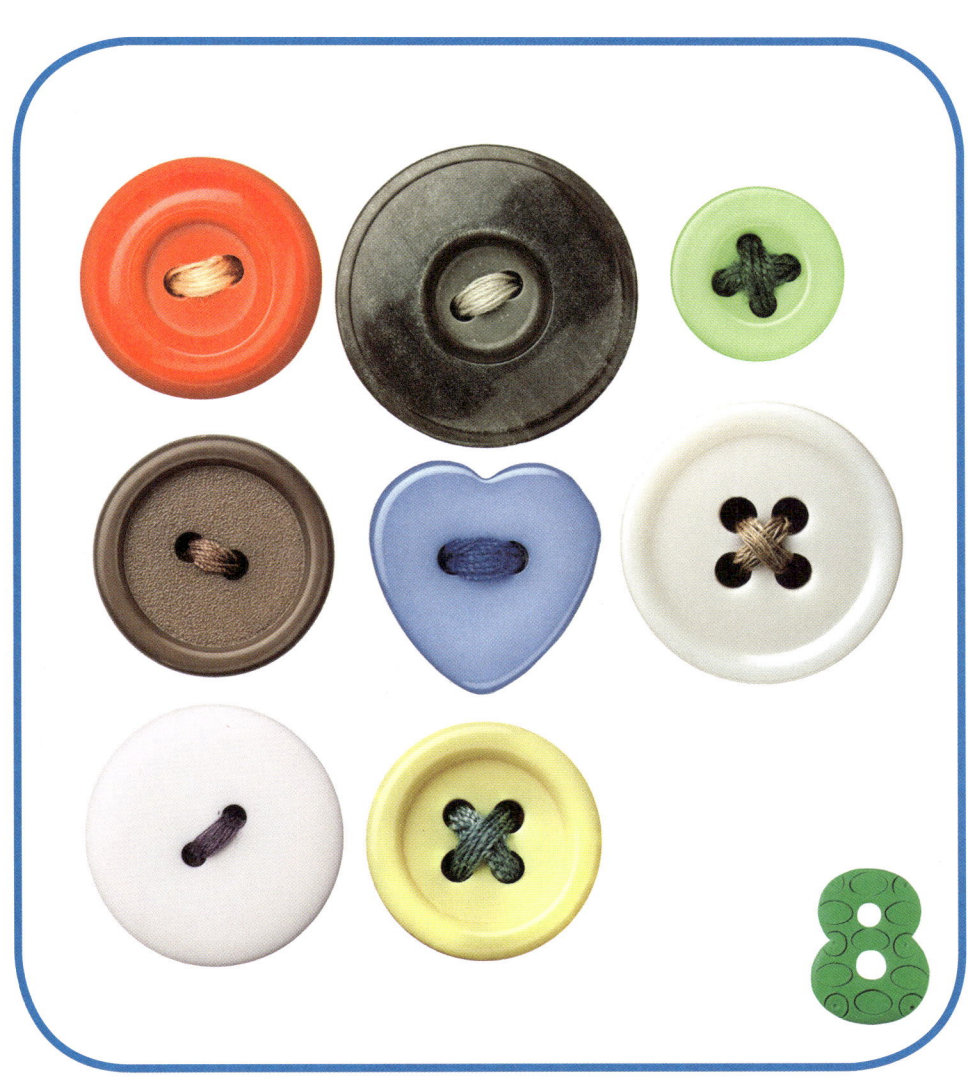

I need eight buttons.

What do you need?

I need keys.

I need nine keys.

What do you need?

I need coins.

I need ten coins.

Let's learn more about Obon.

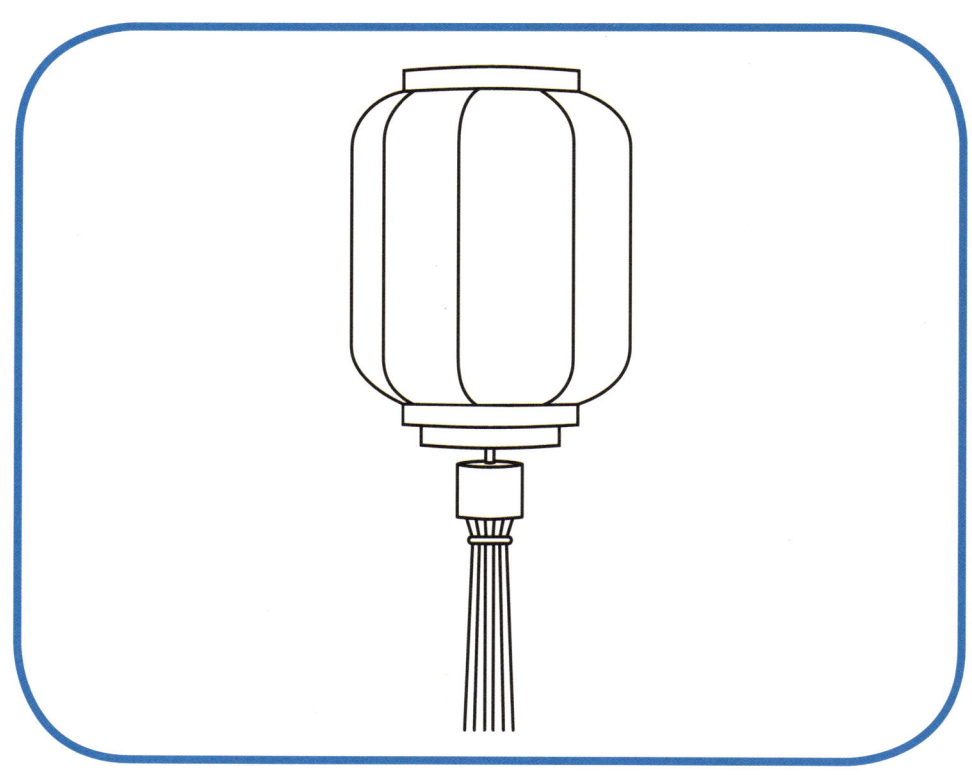

Color the lantern.